W9-CRF-198

HOUGHTON MIFFLIN

Reading

A Legacy of Literacy

Celebrating Traditions

HOUGHTON MIFFLIN

BOSTON • MORRIS PLAINS, NJ

California • Colorado • Georgia • Illinois • New Jersey • Texas

Design, Art Management and Page Production: Kirchoff/Wohlberg, Inc.

ILLUSTRATION CREDITS
4-21 John F. Martin. **23-25, 28-31, 34-38, 52-56** Rosanne Kaloustian.
58-63, 66-75 Robert Casilla.

PHOTOGRAPHY CREDITS
4 Philadelphia Museum of Art/Corbis. **21** Philadelphia Museum of Art/
Corbis. **22** (l) Charles & Josette Lenars/Corbis. **22** (r) The Image Bank.
26 (t) The Image Bank. **26** (b) Charles & Josette Lenars/Corbis. **27** Charles
& Josette Lenars/Corbis. **32-3** Joseph Sohm/Chromosohm/Corbis. **32** (t)
Dave G. Houser/Corbis. **32** (b) Kevin Fleming/Corbis. **33** Kevin Fleming/
Corbis. **39** The Image Bank. **40** (bkg) Gary Retherford/Photo Researchers.
40 Underwood & Underwood/Corbis. **41** Buddy Mays/Corbis. **42** Corbis/
Bettmann. **43** Corbis. **44** Stock Montage. **45** Jerry Jacka Photography.
46 Corbis. **47** Corbis. **48** The Purcell Team/Corbis. **49** (t) The Granger
Collection, New York. **49** (b) Jerry Jacka Photography. **50** Brown Brothers.
51 Jerry Jacka Photography. **57** (t) Gary Retherford/Photo Researchers.
57 (b) Jerry Jacka Photography. **58** Ann Purcell & Carl Purcell/Words &
Pictures/PictureQuest. **75** AFP/Corbis.

Printed in U.S.A.

ISBN: 0-618-03656-3

789-VH-05 04 03 02

Celebrating Traditions

Contents

Grandma's Table

by Penina Adelman

illustrated by John F. Martin

Strategy Focus

What is special about Grandma's table? As you read, **evaluate** the author's memories about her grandmother.

4

Every Friday night, my husband, my children, and I eat at our family table. The table once belonged to my grandmother.

When I was a girl, Grandma lived far away.
My family drove a day and a night to visit her.

When we got there, I ran right into
Grandma's arms. Everyone got a big hug
from Grandma. It was a great place to be.

Then we went into the dining room.
The table was piled high with wonderful food.
"Sit," said Grandma. "Eat."

We ate. We laughed. Grandma told stories.

"I'll never forget the day Grandpa brought
this table from my parents' home,"
Grandma began one story.

"We had such a time getting it up the stairs," she said.

"I've polished it every day since then,"
Grandma said. "I still polish it every day."

The table was as shiny as a butterscotch candy.

Grandma got quiet after that story. "I miss
Grandpa," she said. "He loved our family meals.
Remember how he led the Passover seder?"

We all got quiet for a moment, missing Grandpa.
I still miss him today.

Then Grandma told another story.

"When I was eight, my mother took me out of school to help at home. A woman from the school came to find me. My mother hid me under her family table," said Grandma.

"Later my mother and I laughed about it,"
said Grandma. "But it wasn't funny that I
never went back to school. I'm glad my
grandchild loves school."

"I don't love it *all* the time, Grandma,"
I said. Everyone laughed. They knew I was
joking.

"We don't love school *all* the time, either!"
say my children. Everyone laughs.

Then I tell them more stories around
Grandma's table.

20

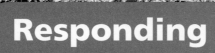

Responding

Think About the Selection

1 What does Grandma do to her table every day?

2 How does the author feel about her Grandpa? Why do you think that?

What Does the Author Feel?

Copy this chart on a piece of paper. Then fill in one more detail from the story that supports what the author feels.

The Author Feels	I know this from these details in the story.
When she was a girl, she liked visiting Grandma.	The author says it was "a great place to be."
The author loved the food that Grandma made.	?

The Mask Makers

by Veronica Freeman Ellis
illustrated by Rosanne Kaloustian

Strategy Focus

A boy goes to Africa to learn a family tradition. As you read, think of **questions** you could ask a friend about this story.

This summer we're visiting my grandfather.
He lives in Monrovia (Mon-**RO**-vee-ah), Liberia
(Lie-**BEAR**-ee-ah). Liberia is a country in Africa.

Here we are in my grandfather's village.
My dad used to live there when he was a boy.

24

My grandfather makes masks.
He carves each mask from one block of wood.

25

In Africa, masks are used for many things.
Sometimes people use them when they get married.

26

Sometimes they use them when a baby is born.
And sometimes they use them when telling stories.

My dad knows how to carve masks too.
His father, my grandfather, taught him.
Now my grandfather teaches me.

I choose a block of wood.
My grandfather shows me what to do.

After many days I have a mask.
I use my mask and tell a story.

My grandfather uses his storytelling mask too.
We all have a good time.

A year has passed.
My grandfather is visiting us in Boston.

Today there's a neighborhood fair.
The fair has rides, crafts, and food.
We're raising money for a playground.

33

My family sells masks that my dad and I made.
My masks don't look as good as my dad's.

People want to buy my dad's masks.
They don't want to buy mine!

But I'm happy anyway.
At least my grandfather likes my masks.

He chooses his favorite one.
Then he uses it to tell a story.

Soon many people gather around my grandfather.
"Once upon a time," he begins.

Responding

Think About the Selection

1 Where does the boy live? Where does his Grandfather live?

2 Tell about two ways the family uses the masks.

Categorize and Classify

In the story, the family members are in two different places. Find some of the things that happen in each place. Write them in a chart like this.

Things That Happen in Liberia	Things That Happen in Boston
Grandfather makes masks.	There is a neighborhood fair.

The Weaver's Gift

by Lee S. Justice
illustrated by Rosanne Kaloustian

Strategy Focus

A Navajo boy tells how his people make rugs. Stop and **summarize** parts of the story as you read. It will help you keep track of the story.

This is the land of the Navajo (**NAHV**-eh-ho) people. Long ago, sheep were brought here.

The Navajo began raising the sheep. They learned to weave with yarn made from the sheep's wool.

Girls learned to weave from their mothers. When the girls grew up, they taught their daughters.

Men and boys helped too. They raised the sheep. They cut the sheep's wool.

The weaver combed out the wool. She pushed
and pulled, using cards with points.

Then the weaver spun the wool. She turned
the wool into yarn.

After that, the weaver gathered plants.
Plants were boiled to make dyes. The dyes
were used to color the yarn.

The weaver set up her loom. In her mind she formed a picture of what she would make. She began weaving the picture into her rug.

Rugs had many kinds of patterns.
Each pattern held special meanings.

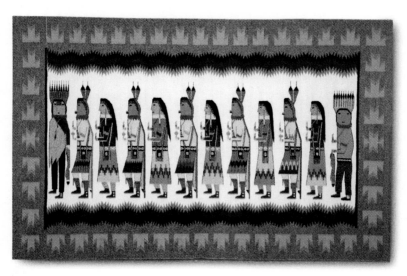

A weaver sang as she sat at the loom. Her songs were woven into the rug. The rug held her thoughts too. It became a part of her.

Navajo weaving began long ago. It is still going on today.

I know these things because I learned them from my Aunt Gloria. She is a weaver. Aunt Gloria came to my school today.

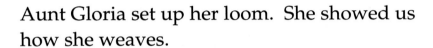

Aunt Gloria set up her loom. She showed us
how she weaves.

My classmates tried weaving.

Then Aunt Gloria said to the class,
"Henry has something to show you."

I held up a rug and said, "This rug was woven by the grandmother of the grandmother of my mother."

Everyone clapped.

Then I said, "This rug is part of my family. That is why it is so beautiful to me."

Responding

1 Among the Navajo people, who teaches the skill of weaving rugs?

2 What details tell you about Aunt Gloria's visit?

Noting Details

Copy the web on a piece of paper. Then write details that complete the idea.

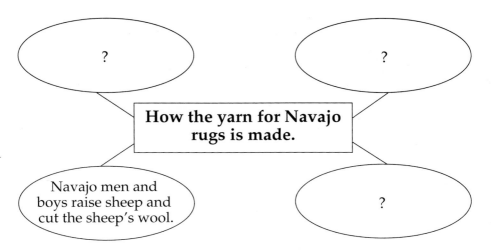

?

?

How the yarn for Navajo rugs is made.

Navajo men and boys raise sheep and cut the sheep's wool.

?

Festival in Valencia

by Anne Miranda

illustrated by
Robert Casilla

Strategy Focus

What are those funny statues in
Valencia? **Monitor** your reading.
Reread to **clarify** any parts you don't
understand.

Ana is visiting her cousin Rocío in Valencia, Spain.

It's time for the yearly festival called *Las Fallas* (**LAS FAH**-yahs).

59

Ana has been to many Mexican festivals at home in Texas.

Rocío says that *Las Fallas* will be very different!

A *falla* (**FAH**-yah) is a big statue. It's made of special paper called *papier-mâché* (**PAY**-per ma-**SHAY**).

Groups of people in Valencia often hire artists to make *fallas*.

Ana's family belongs to one of these groups.

Their *falla* is in pieces on this truck.

Everyone helps put up the *falla*. First, they
unload the pieces. Then they put the pieces
together.

All over Valencia,
other groups are
also putting up
fallas.

64

Fallas often make people laugh. Many *fallas* poke fun at stories in the news. Some are made to look like famous people in Valencia.

65

Ana and her family go to see other *fallas*.
This huge one is in the main plaza.

The group has a party while the *fallas* are being judged. The best *fallas* will win prizes.

The next morning, Ana's family gets exciting
news. Their group's *falla* has won a prize!

Many people have special festival costumes. The
people in Ana's family have had their costumes
for many years. There's an extra one for Ana too.

This year, Rocío's mother has been chosen to pick up the prize for the whole group.

Next comes a parade. People in the group love
to show off their winning *falla*.

On the last night, Ana is in for a big surprise.
First, the fire fighters spray the buildings.
This is so the buildings won't burn. Then
they set fire to the *fallas* all over Valencia!

Everyone else is cheering, but Ana is shocked!

Rocío explains that the *fallas* are always burned. It is the tradition.

Next year, their new *fallas* will be just
as wonderful!

Responding

Think About the Selection

1 What is a *falla* ?

2 Besides making a *falla*, groups in Valencia celebrate this festival in other ways. Write ways they celebrate.

Main Idea and Details

Copy the chart on a piece of paper. Write two supporting details for the second main idea.

Main Ideas	Supporting Details
Many groups plan for *Las Fallas*.	1. The groups hire artists to make *fallas* that will win prizes. 2. They show off their *fallas* in a parade all over Valencia.
At the festival's end, the *fallas* are burned.	1.　　　　? 2.　　　　?